# Savoring Christmas

31 Devotions to Prepare Your Heart for the
Messiah

Stacy Voss

# Table of Contents

# Acknowledgements

With humble gratitude, I dedicate this book to the following:

My Masterminds and dear friends, Dianne Daniels and Robbie Iobst. This book would not exist if it weren't for your keen eyes, but more than that, your encouragement and love.

My Soul Sisters and the many, many people who have prayed me through a season that I never would have withstood had it not been for your countless prayers. There is no way I can possibly begin to say how grateful I am.

The many "elves" who showered me with love and allowed me to see what Christmas is really about. Your compassion and generosity boosted my spirits and provided for us in real and indescribable ways. Thank you.

To everyone who has encouraged me with my writing over the years and inspired me to keep going, thank you. I don't do this for you, yet you help me keep doing this.

Mom and Dad: thank you. You've always been there. I know that's no small thing.

To the Charts: the tears well and a knot forms in my throat, for I am so overcome in gratitude to you. You have given me a home, a refuge, family, and a demonstration of a much better way of living. Words can't express what you've done or how deeply I cherish you.

And of course, my kids that I am so very fortunate to be "Mama" to and get to be a part of their lives. I'm so very proud of you. My love runs deeper for you than you'll ever know.

# Author's Note

I know you're smack-dab in the middle of a busy season, of buying presents, baking cookies, or doing a million different things. It is my sincerest hope that the words on these pages will bring you calm, peace, and perspective, and that through them, our hearts may be fully prepared to celebrate the birth of our Messiah.

You'll notice there is a devotion for every day throughout the month of December. I tried stopping on Christmas Day, yet I just couldn't. After all, how could we spend so many days preparing for such a magnificent event and then stop on the day we get to revel in it? I just had to keep writing! In those extra days, you'll find some prompts to stop and say thanks, as well as some things to help prepare your heart for the upcoming year.

Use this book in the way that best suits you. Some of you will turn it into a journal of sorts, with notes, prayers and reflections jotted throughout. Others of you will be doing well just to read the devotional each day, but might not have time to make it to the "Stop and Savor" section. That's perfectly fine, too. You aren't being graded, and this in no way is meant to heap on guilt. So let's commit right now to putting the shame to rest, and instead to dig in in a way that will allow us to savor Christmas like never before and to prepare our hearts for Immanuel—God with Us!

Stacy Voss

# December 1st

## Scarfing Versus Savoring

I've heard of fast eaters, but my black lab takes the cake (literally!). She can finish off her dinner in twenty-three seconds flat.

Twenty-three seconds!

It happens so fast that I have a hard time remembering if she's been fed or not. The same is true of her. She comes begging within minutes of eating, apparently forgetting that she just scarfed down her meal.

I laugh and tell her to lie down, but sometimes I look at her and see myself. No, I don't have fur, nor do I walk on all fours. But I am prone to forget the things I do in haste. Sometimes I touch the head of my toothbrush to check if it's wet since I can't remember if I brushed or not. Other times I eat lunch while I work and then struggle to recall if I ate or not. And then there are the times when I race from one activity to the next, dashing so quickly that I only remember feeling rushed while forgetting who I spent time with. The calendar fills and the memory fades.

Schedules bulge this time of year with pageants, baking cookies, addressing cards, and buying presents. If we aren't careful, our Decembers could be defined by rushing from one activity to the next.

They could be, but they don't have to.

Yes, our days might be busier than normal, but it can also be a season of heart training. Matthew 6:21 says, "For where your treasure is, there your heart will be also." After the angels echoed carols of praise throughout the skies and the shepherds came to see the newborn king, "Mary treasured up all these things and pondered them in her heart" (Luke 2:19). She undoubtedly savored that moment and her heart was fully present in the grandeur of God's miracle.

So many things fight to earn the spot of being most treasured in our hearts this time of year. What will you most treasure?

# Stop and Savor

1) What are some things you treasure about the Christmas season? Some examples are looking at lights or seeing *The Nutcracker*. Perhaps you enjoy being known for finding the perfect gift or baking the best cookies. What do you most want to treasure this season?

2) Deuteronomy 8:10 says, "When you have eaten and are satisfied, praise the LORD your God for the good land he has given you." I normally pray before a meal, but what if the time of gratitude came *afterwards*? Would that cause you to savor the food more? Give it a try today and say thanks after each snack and meal.

3) Create a "treasure box" for this Christmas season. Perhaps you'll use a small bucket or container, or maybe a gift bag. Jot down things throughout December as you ponder them, and then place them in your treasure box. Do you think you can fill it by Christmas Day?

---

Savoring leads to creating a treasure.

"For where your heart is, your

treasure is also."

~Matthew 6:21

---

# December 2nd

## Overwhelmed With Wonder

I remember watching my kids 'ooh' and 'ahh' this time of year when they were young. They'd look around the room, staring at the lights in fascination and sheer amazement. It was a season of awe and wonder.

It still is for some, but for most of us it looks very different now than when we were kids. The fretting and to-do lists trump the awe, relegating the "wonder" to thoughts such as:

"I wonder how I'll have time to bake all the cookies, and buy all the presents."

"I wonder how I'll be able to pay for the gifts I bought."

"I wonder if I'll get along with the in-laws this year."

"I wonder if I'll get something good. It has to compete."

Whoa! Compete? Yes, those were the words my daughter muttered one December evening, wanting assurance that what she received would rank up there with the laptop her friend was getting (to which I quickly assured her she didn't need to worry since her presents wouldn't even come close).

Micayla and I sat down on her bed as I reminded her of the true meaning of Christmas. I told her about the one whose birth had been predicted long before, about a young unmarried woman who found out she was going to have a baby, and about a sacrifice of love so deep and pure that it bypasses all understanding. Perhaps she learned something from it (but probably not since she was still sulking about the lack of a laptop). Whether or not the talk meant anything to her, it reminded me of one powerful truth: Christmas doesn't have anything to do with what's under the tree.

Instead, Christmas has everything to do with who is in your heart.

We can laugh and chuckle at the words of a child. Of course we know Christmas isn't about competing (or at least we'll say we know that, but the way we act might be a different story). Yet the other "wonders" of the season—the wondering if we'll tackle everything that must be done before the ominous deadline—is as far from the meaning of Christmas as expecting what we receive to compare to what our friends and family will get.

Mark 9:15 gives us a taste of the wonder involved with beholding Christ, our Messiah:

"As soon as all the people saw Jesus, **they were overwhelmed with wonder and ran to greet him**" (emphasis mine).

That is my prayer for you and me this season. May we slow long enough to see Jesus, and when we do, may we be overwhelmed with wonder. Let us run to greet Him and invite Him in–even if there are cobwebs in the corners of our house or chaos throughout our lives.

The wonder still lives, at least if we let it.

Christmas doesn't have anything to do with what's under the tree. It has everything to do with who is in your heart.

# Stop and Savor

1) Think back to what Christmas was like as a child. What were some of your favorite memories?

2) When was the last time you were overwhelmed with wonder? Did you outgrow that sense of awe?

3) Imagine seeing Jesus. What type of wonder would you feel in His presence? Pray and ask Jesus to let you see Him more this Christmas season—no, not in a literal sense, but to see His touch and His presence throughout your days. What if you were to ask to be overwhelmed with wonder by Him?

# December 3rd

## The Scent of Death

My jammie pants ended up in the dryer. Again. At 5'10", I have a hard enough time getting them to reach my ankles without having them shrink. Not wanting yet another Capri-looking bottom, I Googled ways to un-shrink clothes.

One source suggested soaking them in water with a capful of baby shampoo. *It can't hurt,* I thought as I put the item on my shopping list.

A few days later, I started the Make-My-Pants-Long-Again project. I filled the kitchen sink with lukewarm water and added the shampoo. Nostalgia swept over me as its unmistakable aroma reached my nose. *How many times had I bathed my Bubba in that sink when he was little?* I recalled his first baths in that large, white basin, fearful that I'd drop his small, wriggly body onto its hard sides. I "saw" him as he grew over the months, laughing hysterically as he soaked everyone and everything.

"Mom, what are you doing?" my daughter asked, snapping me out of my flashback.

Dropping the pants I was cradling, I sheepishly replied, "I, uh, um, I'm making my pants long again."

Scents have the power to move us in time, merging the present with the past. But could it also predict the future?

We all know of the gifts the three wise men presented to Jesus, but what shocked me was to hear a description of myrrh. Myrrh's main use back in Jesus' day was to treat wounds and pain. It was also the "essential ingredient in ancient Egyptian funeral rites."[1]

Gold and frankincense were fitting gifts for the infant king. But myrrh, reeking of its scent of death? Did its odor override the sweet aroma of the newborn, drawing them back to when one of their loved ones was buried?

Just like shrinking your pants can't be reversed, baby shampoo or not, the myrrh hinted at something that was already set in motion that couldn't be undone. Death was on its way.

---

The myrrh hinted at something that was already set in motion that couldn't be undone. Death was on its way.

---

While Christmas is a time of celebration, let's stop long enough to soak in the aroma of the myrrh, for the bitterness makes the rejoicing that much sweeter.

# Stop and Savor

1) What smells are nostalgic for you? Why?

2) How would you respond if someone gave a perfectly healthy newborn an obituary notice?

3) What was offered to Jesus during the crucifixion that He refused (Mark 15:23)?

4) According to John 19:25, who was near the cross during Jesus' crucifixion? Do you think she remembered the gift of myrrh given at Jesus' birth or smelled it as it was offered to Jesus as He hung on the cross?

5) Leave cookies in the oven too long or overcook a bag of microwave popcorn. Soak in the pungent aroma as a reminder of the not-so-savory gift given to Jesus.

# December 4th

## Remembering the Words

My son stood in the front of the auditorium, dressed in his Sunday best. It was his big moment. All he had to do was stand there with his preschool friends and sing the songs they had rehearsed every morning for the past two months.

The music began playing. One boy belted out the words, his voice prevailing over the rest. Of course there was the girl that picked up her skirt and covered her head with it. Fortunately "loud guy's" singing muffled the crowd's laughter. And then there was my Bubba standing perfectly still on the first row. Let me reiterate: *perfectly* still. His arms remained at his side. His eyes shifted a bit as he looked at the other kids, yet his mouth stayed shut. The words escaped him, and therefore couldn't escape him!

Can you relate? I sure can. So many times I learn a song, but something causes me to forget its words. I find this especially true during Christmas. Yes, I stumble over the lesser-known verses of various carols, but there is one song in particular I forget. When I say I forget it, I'm not referring to just a few lines of the third stanza. I'm talking about the entire song, title, chorus, take-away message and all.

It's Mary's song. Here are some of the lyrics: "My soul glorifies the Lord and my spirit rejoices in God my Savior" (Luke 1:46-47). Sure, I've never memorized these words verbatim, but my heart echoes the sentiment frequently as I praise and thank God.

But something often happens as I sing. Sometimes it's the glare of the lights as I stand in front of others, my insecurities and self-doubt replacing my trust in God. Other times it's the torrents of life that mute my ballad. If I'm not careful, I'll focus on those hardships and forget there ever was a song. My praise turns to accusations of "Why, God?"

Mary could have asked why: why did God choose her, why did she have to have her firstborn while she was so far away from her family, why was the Messiah born in a stinky stable? Her list of whys could have been endless, but instead of questions blurting from her mouth, we hear a song of love and devotion.

December is a time of song. Children have their pageants, carolers stroll down the lane, and the music over P.A. systems is cranked up louder than normal. Stop and listen. Remember the words. Then commit to singing the song of praise all year long.

# Stop and Savor

1) Read Mary's song (Luke 1:46-55) and Zechariah's song (Luke 1:67-79). What differences and similarities do you find between the two?

2) Pick one line from Mary's or Zechariah's song. Commit it to memory. If your capacity to memorize is anything like mine, you might want to choose "holy is his name" for its power and brevity (Luke 1:49b). Consider writing it on a card and placing it in a prominent place you'll see every day such as on your mirror, desk, or the dashboard of your car. Let your heart sing it every day.

3) Whenever you hear a Christmas carol, remember to "sing" praises to God.

# December 5th

## It Isn't Supposed to Be This Way

How many times have you told yourself "it isn't supposed to be this way?" Maybe it was when you were about to have a mental breakdown in the store as you scrambled to buy one of the few toys left on the shelf. Perhaps you thought it after snapping at your kids, knowing the real problem was your sheer exhaustion from attending too many Christmas parties.

So often we overschedule in December and feel frenetic, but what about the times when we're lonely due to the loss of a loved one or from being apart from family.

"It isn't supposed to be this way," we silently scream when we hear our grown kids won't be coming home, making our reality that much harder as we couple it with unmet expectations.

My guess is this sentiment has been expressed since the first Christmas.

Think of Joseph knocking on doors, crying out for anyone who would assist him. "Please, sir.

My wife . . . Yes, I know everything is full, but the baby's on its way. It's not just any baby, either."

Can you fathom Joseph's emotions? He was the head of the house, longing to provide and protect as God has built into every man, and yet he watched as his wife writhe in pain without even a soft place to lie down. *God, surely you don't want your son to be born like this!*

Did Mary have her, "it isn't supposed to be this way" moments, too? Her childhood dreams of being a mom never looked like this. Maybe she always pictured her own mother there for the birth of her firstborn, yet there she was, in a musky stable, giving birth to the Most High.

A prince. In a place built for animals.

The Messiah, as a helpless baby.

It isn't supposed to be this way.

Or is it?

Today is the only day that I ask that you make sure you read the accompanying questions, for in them you'll find the answer to the statement so many of us have muttered.

> "The LORD Almighty has sworn, 'Surely, as I have planned, so it will be, and as I have purposed, so it will happen."
> Isaiah 14:24

# Stop and Savor

1) Is there anything in your life this time of year that makes you say, "It isn't supposed to be this way?" If so, is it because of your schedule and priorities, or is it beyond your control?

2) Proverbs 3:5-6 says, "Trust in the LORD with all your heart and lean not on your own understanding; in all your ways submit to him, and he will make your paths straight." Is there anything in your life that doesn't make sense, yet you are willing to trust in the Lord rather than your own abilities?

3) How do the following verses help answer the question "Or is it?"

"I say, 'My purpose will stand, and I will do all that I please.' From the east I summon a bird of prey; from a far-off land, a man to fulfill my purpose. What I have said, that I will bring about; what I have planned, that I will do." Isaiah 46:10-11

4) Do these verses provide you any comfort or encouragement to your "it isn't supposed to be this way" thoughts?

# December 6th

## O' Christmas Tree

Okay, I'm going out on a limb here (excuse the pun!) as we chat about Christmas trees. Many believe they came from pagan roots (oops! That one was accidental). I don't doubt they did, yet I believe it's possible to see the tree as something much more than that.

To me, the Christmas tree is the perfect juxtaposition. Blessings and curses. Grace and shame. Life and death. Let me explain.

Mary wrapped the tiny newborn Messiah in swaddling clothes and then laid Him in a manger: a feeding box for animals! Think about how horrific it must have been to put a baby in a trough, especially considering the Jewish laws and customs. Leviticus 11:7-8 says, "And the pig, though it has a divided hoof, does not chew the cud; it is unclean for you. You must not eat their meat or touch their carcasses; they are unclean for you."

Let that settle in. Jews couldn't eat pigs. Nor could they touch their carcasses, yet the promised Savior was placed in a feeding vestibule that could have been for the animals His people were forbidden to eat. It was as unthinkable as placing a newborn in an old toilet. Yet the unthinkable happened, an act of love to care for the newborn Messiah that reeked of shame.

Was the manger a foreshadowing of Jesus' death? The one born surrounded by wood would die hanging from wood. The similarities between his birth and death don't end there.

---

Born surrounded by wood. Died on wood.
Born in shame. Died in shame.

---

Deuteronomy 21: 22-23a says, "If someone has committed a crime worthy of death and is executed and hung on a tree, the body must not remain hanging from the tree overnight. You must bury the body that same day, for anyone who is hung is cursed in the sight of God."

I used to think "hung on a tree" was limited to something involving a noose, but as I've researched its original meaning, it's clear this verse simply meant any version of capital punishment involving wood in an outdoor forum. It was a disgraceful act, so much so that it brought God's curse.

The shame of being placed in a manger paled in comparison with being hung on a cross, of having birds land on Christ's dying body without the ability to swat them off. Anyone who cared to observe could watch Christ's breaths grow more and more shallow, celebrating in a gruesome way the fleeing of life.

I don't know the history behind a Christmas tree and honestly I don't want to. Instead, I let my tree serve as a reminder. I feel the wood (or the plastic, as is usually the case in my house), and let it remind me of the manger and cross. I feel the needles, their tips poking at my skin, and remember the one who came knowing His life would end with a crown of thorns pressed into His brow. And on the many years when something goes awry as I try to set up my tree and end up leaning it against the wall—a sad Charlie Brown sight that makes me want to apologize for its appearance—I remember the shame that decorated Christ's birth and death.

"Oh Christmas tree, Oh Christmas tree,
You'll ever be unchanging"
~ O Christmas Tree, Ernst Anschutz

# Stop and Savor

1) What is the most expensive gift you ever bought someone? Did you wrap it beautifully, or place it in a used, raggedy gift bag?

2) Recall your most embarrassing moment or something that caused you great shame. Would you willingly relive that experience? Would you purposefully subject yourself to something that you knew others viewed as shameful?

3) Why do you think God allowed Jesus to be born in a manger? What does that tell you about Christ's character (i.e. Does He seem proud, lowly, capable, etc.)? How does Philippians 2:5-8 add to that description?

# December 7th

## You Got Me A What?!?

There's always *that* present, you know, the one you can't wait to tear in to. It could be the one that's been on the list since December 26th of the previous year, or the one wrapped so beautifully it undoubtedly holds something exquisite. Or, it might be the one that's talked about so much that you just have to know what it is.

That's how it was for me when I was twelve. My parents kept talking about a gift they knew I'd love. I couldn't believe it—my parents just weren't known for their gifting abilities. The glisten in their eyes convinced me I was about to receive something beyond my expectations.

Christmas morning came and I quickly learned which one *it* was: the one that caused a reaction in my parents whenever I grabbed it. It was also the one I wasn't allowed to open until there weren't any more presents under the tree.

I tore into my gifts. I'm sure they were fabulous, but I don't remember any of them since I was so anxious to open my special present.

Finally, it was time. I ripped off the wrapping paper and found a fire extinguisher. A fire extinguisher!

Every girl's dream come true, right?

Wrong!

My parents had previously assumed that if there were ever a fire in the basement (where my bedroom was), I could simply push on the plastic bubble covering the window well and escape the flames. My mom had an unfortunate episode that proved their theory wrong. While cleaning the window one day, she got trapped in the small, spider-infested cage. She pushed with all her might, but the landscaping rocks on the edges of the bubble were too heavy. Figuring a grown adult couldn't get out through the bubble, my parents saw the need to arm me with something to keep me safe.

They beamed with pride for giving me something that could save my life. I, on the other hand, wallowed, disappointed after receiving something so practical and contrary to my expectations.

Centuries ago, a group of mistreated people had an escape plan: someone from their ranks would free them from their oppression. He'd probably even make the tyrants pay for what they'd done.

Before long, they found themselves trapped in a cage of sorts with nothing more than a fire extinguisher. A disappointing gift that failed to meet any of their expectations.

A Messiah. One to deliver and redeem. A baby born in the lowliest of places.

That baby would grow into a man. He would be humble and meek, but He would also ransom and save.

Years after the you-got-me-a-what?!? Christmas, flames erupted in my kitchen. Of course you know what I did: I raced to my room and grabbed the fire extinguisher.

The thing I hadn't wanted was the thing I most desperately needed.

# Stop and Savor

1) How do you view Jesus? You can be totally honest here, for even God can handle it. Do you see him as nothing more than a fire extinguisher, a thing of disappointment, something to grab when life heats up, the person who has changed your everything, or do you fall somewhere in between?

2) How does your response to the previous question make you feel? This isn't to cause shame or guilt, but to ask if you like the perspective you have of Jesus. If you don't, what might you do to change that?

3) Isaiah 53:3 says of Jesus, "He was despised and rejected by mankind, a man of suffering, and familiar with pain. Like one from whom people

hide their faces he was despised, and we held him in low esteem."

Your view of Jesus doesn't impact
Jesus' view of you.

# December 8<sup>th</sup>

## God, Sitting on a Curb

"Why did we have to walk today?" Gabe whined as we made the short trek home from school. Well, the normally short-trek, I should say. He's my energetic bundle who is always excited to bike or run, yet this particular day was different. Each step was cumbersome and tears flowed faster than his legs moved.

There wasn't a reason for the change of attitude. Nothing bad happened at school and there was plenty to look forward to at home. It just was one of those days.

After struggling down the first of five blocks, Gabe just gave up, plopping himself down on the street corner. I stood there for a bit, realizing whatever was troubling Gabe wasn't going to disappear quickly. Without a word, I sat down next to him. He obviously didn't want to talk, so I just held onto the leash of our black lab while he fiddled with a blade of grass.

Cars slowed to make sure we were okay. Strange expressions plagued faces. And yet, we just sat there in utter silence.

A few minutes later Gabe popped up and said, "Okay, let's go." No explanation was given and none needed. We walked the rest of the way home without incident.

I can't explain the change in demeanor. Maybe it was just the chance to sit and rest. Or maybe my presence without condemnation soothed him. I can't say for sure, but what I can say is that our time on that street corner taught me something.

I learned the meaning of Christmas.

There have been countless times in my life when I longed to know I wasn't alone. It didn't matter if I was married or single, there were—and are—those moments of feeling isolated and unknown. The best Christmas present is the realization we aren't.

The angel let Mary know what her son's name would be, a name sent straight from heaven: Immanuel. God with us.[2]

The loneliness broke as royalty clothed itself in humble flesh and allowed itself to feel every emotion that we do.

Yet we know what happened to that flesh many years down the road as it was ripped and torn when God With Us went to the cross.

The incredible, magnificent gift was no more. Or so they thought for a brief period of time. But then, a promise:

> "Nevertheless, I tell you the truth: it is to
> your advantage that I go away, for if I do not
> go away, the Helper will not come to you.
> But if I go, I will send him to you."
> John 16:7 (ESV)

First, the tremendous gift of royalty here with us. Then a promise of something even better. Something guaranteed to take up residence in you to lead, guide, comfort, and maybe even sit with you on the side of a street in your times of despair, joy, sorrow and everything in between.

# Stop and Savor

1) Imagine you're having tea with the queen. What do you think the conversation would be like? Do you think it would mostly be about politics or about Her Highness? Do you think she would take a great interest in your daily life, and if so, do you think she could relate to it?

2) We might not be able to relate to royalty, but there is a King of Kings who fully understands us. How does that make you feel?

3) The following is a list of words other Bible translations use instead of Helper in John 16:7. Jot next to each word what it means to have someone with that characteristic residing within you.

- Advocate

# Savoring Christmas

- Comforter

- Companion

- Counselor

- Holy Spirit

- Intercessor

- Strengthener

# December 9th

## Freedom from my Don'ts

I'm not Santa, but I'm definitely known for making my list and checking it twice (twice an hour, that is). But unlike that jolly guy, my list isn't limited just to what to get others. It also includes the many tasks that seem to multiply during the Christmas season. You know: buy flour, butter and sugar in bulk for the many cookies that will be baked and delivered. Stand in line at the post office for several hours. Attempt to figure out how to stretch pennies to buy everyone that thing they've always wanted.

This past Christmas, there were a lot of things I never did. Here are just a few:

- I didn't bake cookies. Not a single one. My kids didn't cover the floors in icing, and we didn't spend hours driving around delivering treats.
- I didn't send out Christmas cards. Again. Our family joke is "what do you get when you cross a mailman and a writer?" "I don't know, but it isn't a Christmas card."

- I didn't buy gifts for most of my friends. In fact, I only bought my husband something really small.
- We didn't drive around for hours looking at lights. Then again, we also didn't get lost or get into an argument over which direction to go in order to find the best lit house.
- We didn't bundle up and head to an outdoor skating rink.

I never meant to have my list of don'ts. I hadn't planned cancelling the very things that had become our tradition. Yet for as long as my list of things that didn't get accomplished is, the list that truly matters is what I did manage to do:

- I savored time with family and friends. Our time together was filled with love and laughter rather than stress and anxiety.
- I came to better appreciate the gift of Christmas, something I only could do by being more rested and less rushed. I let myself truly enter into the season rather than being a spectator to it.

Chances are no one else will notice if you put up the extra string of garland on your step railings, or if you bake three kinds of cookies or ten. So let's give ourselves a gift this year and declare freedom from the don'ts.

# Stop and Savor

1) What is one thing you normally do every Christmas season? If you're anything like me, your list will probably be much longer than just one thing.

2) What might happen if you didn't do it this year? What could you gain by skipping it?

3) Galatians 5:6b says, "The only thing that counts is faith expressing itself through love." How does this verse connect to relinquishing the feelings of what we "should" do? How does that impact you?

# December 10th

## Immanuel

I can't wait for my husband to play Joe Satriani's song "Always with You, Always with Me," for me on his guitar this Christmas. I listened to this song repeatedly years ago as the wordless melody somehow promised what the title claims. Always with you. Always with me.

Isn't it alluring to have someone in our lives who will always be there with us? Oh how I longed for someone who could accept my serious side, my happy-go-lucky moments, the fearless me and the parts of me that shiver and whimper like a frightened little puppy.

Always with you. Always with me.

What a grand dream. I think I would've settled for just a "Hey, I kind of like you and I might stick around for a bit" type of Joe or maybe even an "I'll give you some of the attention you desperately crave, but I can't promise if I'll stick around if you don't meet all of my needs."

Sort of with you. Sort of with me.

The story of Christmas is nestled in the beautiful backdrop of truth. No kindas, sort-ofs, or anything of the sort. This is the always with you, always with me romanticism our hearts could never even dare dream about. Savor the words you have heard so many times before. Allow them to fall afresh in a way like never before.

"This is how the birth of Jesus Christ came about: His mother Mary was pledged to be married to Joseph, but before they came together, she was found to be with child through the Holy Spirit. Because Joseph her husband was a righteous man and did not want to expose her to public disgrace, he had in mind to divorce her quietly.

But after he had considered this, an angel of the Lord appeared to him in a dream and said, 'Joseph son of David, do not be afraid to take Mary home as your wife, because what is conceived in her is from the Holy Spirit. She will give birth to a son, and you are to give him the name Jesus, because he will save his people from their sins.'

All this took place to fulfill what the Lord had said through the prophet: 'The virgin will be with child and will give birth to a son, and they will call him Immanuel'—which

means, 'God with us."
Matthew 1:18-23

God with us. I want to challenge you this Christmas season to experience God's presence in a way you never have previously. December usually is a month in which we run from one Christmas party to the next, go to umpteen different stores, send cards, wrap presents and find ourselves beat and exhausted. In the midst of the celebrations, it can also be a time of increased loneliness, depression or disappointment. Where, we might ask, is God in the middle of that?

Please just look. Immanuel, God with us, looked very different that first Christmas than many expected. While hopes of a king coming in power to victoriously save the people from oppression kept most looking for jewels and crowns, the true Messiah humbly lay in a smelly feeding trough. And while we look for relief from our pain, suffering or loneliness, Immanuel may appear very differently to us this year. Perhaps it will be through the prompting to buy dinner for a stranger or sacrifice something that affects you deeply for the benefit of another. Perhaps Immanuel will come to you through the provision of a friend, meal, or touch.

In this world of relativism, one truth still remains. God *is* with us.

# Stop and Savor

1) Spend some time today looking for Jesus. At the end of the day, write down a few places you saw Him or His glory. Some examples might be the touch of a friend, a sunset, a phone call, etc.

2) Matthew 28:19-20 says, "Therefore go and make disciples of all nations, baptizing them in the name of the Father and of the Son and of the Holy Spirit, and teaching them to obey everything I have commanded you. **And surely I am with you always,** to the very end of the age" (emphasis mine).

   How does the fact that you are loved in an "always with you" way affect you? Does it compel you to live differently?

3) What can you do to reach out to someone who might be lonely this time of year? Perhaps there

is a widow, a single mom, or an elderly person with no family around who could desperately use a little reminder that society hasn't forgotten about them. How can you help fill that role?

# December 11<sup>th</sup>

## No Parking Spots

What's harder than finding the perfect gift for Aunt Hilda? A parking spot at the mall in December. The madness can turn even the most gentle, law-abiding citizen into a crazed maniac.

While I usually have my shopping done early, there was one mall trip that was unavoidable last December. A car happened to be leaving, so my husband and I waited in the parking lot aisle as they backed out. Apparently they went too slowly, for a cop came barreling by in his patrol car and clipped our mirror. Yes, a cop. I laughed hysterically as the officer called his supervisor to report himself.

Like I said, trying times bring out odd reactions in each of us. Imagine Joseph's response as every innkeeper turned him away. There wouldn't be any "waiting in the aisles," for no one would be leaving that night.

A scene from *Oliver Twist* comes to mind when I think of Joseph looking for a place for Mary to give birth. My imagination conjures up images of inn-keepers laughing at Joseph's request for lodging in much the same way as when Oliver asked for more food. Can't you just hear it? "Please, sir, could I please have a room?"

"A room! A room? Hey boys, listen up, he wants a room!" a man snorts as he bursts into laughter knowing that all of the lodging filled up days earlier.

So as you wrack your brain trying to figure out what to give Aunt Hilda,

Or see a police officer patrolling the mall parking lot,

Or wait forever in said lot for an available spot,

Think about Joseph in his hunt.

And then think about your own search. Have you searched and found God?

Are you ready to do your own Oliver Twist impersonation: "Please, God, I want some more. More of you."

# Stop and Savor

1) Are you searching for the right things this Christmas?

2) The following verses tell us some things we can ask for more of. What are they?

> "But he gives us more grace. That is why Scripture says: 'God opposes the proud but shows favor to the humble." James 4:6

> "And this is my prayer: that your love may abound more and more in knowledge and depth of insight, so that you may be able to discern what is best and may be pure and blameless for the day of Christ, filled with the fruit of righteousness that comes through Jesus Christ—to the glory and praise of God." Philippians 1:9-11

"We ought always to thank God for you, brothers and sisters, and rightly so, because your faith is growing more and more, and the love all of you have for one another is increasing." 2 Thessalonians 1:3

4) If you have the time, patience or self-control, go to the mall today. While you look for a parking spot, spend the time in prayer, asking for more of God's presence, direction and influence in your life (but watch out for policemen!).

# December 12ᵗʰ

## Semantics

He moved more slowly than he used to, old age settling into the disappointment housed in the marrow of his bones. How long had they begged for a child?

He shook his head, attempting to toss the ache away yet again as he prepared to enter the temple. No room for condemning God there.

As he prepared to burn the incense, an angel appeared. "Do not be afraid, Zechariah; your prayer has been heard. Your wife Elizabeth will bear you a son, and you are to call him John" (Luke 1:13).

A son? A son! His prayers had been heard! So many thoughts raced through his mind: Was he imagining? How would he tell Elizabeth? Was the incense playing tricks on him?

Out of all the unspoken questions, one reached his tongue: "How can I be sure of this?" (Luke 1:18).

Fast forward six months. The scene is different this time. No elaborate preparations have been made. No encounters predicted. Just a regular day once again.

Until.

"Greetings, you who are highly favored! The Lord is with you" (Luke 1:28).

Gabriel's words—his very presence, actually—unsettled Mary. Of course this young woman became frightened, but the angel's words reassured her. Well, mostly. The part about "Do not be afraid, Mary; you have found favor with God" did, but then he went on to tell her that she'd give birth to the Son of the Most High (Luke 1:30-33).

Notice the drastic difference in her response as compared to Zechariah's: "How will this be . . . since I am a virgin?" (Luke 1:34).

Mary and Elizabeth were unlikely candidates of getting pregnant. Elizabeth was well beyond child-bearing years, but her odds were better than Mary's. Yet the priest, Zechariah, questioned the angel, demanding a sign. Mary, however, accepted the angel's word as true, simply requiring a God-style birds and bees talk.

The older priest questioned "How can I be sure of this?" while the young girl replied "May it be to me as you have said" (Luke 1:38).

Both received a gift when they were visited by the one who stands in the presence of God. One, with his scholarly wisdom, questioned it. The other, in her humble state, embraced it.

If God, Gabriel or the Holy Spirit were to tell you something, whom would you most be like: Mary or Zechariah?

# Stop and Savor

1) Are you more like Zechariah in that you'll believe something once you've seen it or need further verification of it, or are you like Mary? Which do you want to be more like? Think of one thing you can do today to help you in that goal?

2) The King James Version gives a different twist to Zechariah's words (and apparently his name, too!): "And Zacharias said unto the angel, 'Whereby shall I know this? For I am an old man, and my wife well stricken in years" (Luke 1:18). The word "know" comes from the Greek word *ginōskō,* which is the same word used in Matthew 7:23. Read its context, and then ask yourself what ramifications there will be for living your life wanting to be sure of God, yet never really knowing God or being known by Him.

3) Do you hear the Christmas story and think it's just that: a story? Does it seem too far-fetched to believe a virgin could become pregnant or that the Son of God would be born in a manger? Sounds pretty crazy, right? Well, if you're having a hard time believing it was real, don't be scared to tell Jesus.

# December 13<sup>th</sup>

## Foreshadowing

My creative writing teacher always challenged us to employ foreshadowing, giving readers hints at what was about to come. It was difficult for me to do because I never knew where my story would take me since I simply penned words as they came to me.

---

Your actions today foreshadow your tomorrows.

---

If I'm not careful, I tend to live the same way. I don't know where my "story" will lead, so I make choices without weighing the long-term consequences. It's only once I look back that I see the foreshadowing, the writing on my heart, that shaped where I am today. Whether I notice it or not, my actions today are a foreshadowing of my tomorrows.

It's not a new concept. In fact, it happened on the night of Jesus' birth. The only difference is that

God was very much aware of the present *and* the future. One such example revolves around some of the lowest ranked members of society.

The first people to hear of Christ's birth were shepherds, who were considered to be some of the lowliest people in that day's culture. Shepherds had to sleep in open fields, unprotected from the elements. They were so low in the ranks that they were expected to risk their own lives if something threatened an animal in their fold.

Compare that to the birth of the Messiah. We've already discussed how unthinkable it must have been to put the newborn king in a stinky manger. The Christ child was born in a lowly setting, and the theme of humility continued throughout His life. Although He could have demanded prestige or recognition, He never did. In fact, the only time He allowed people to fully worship and celebrate Him was while he was seated upon the back of a humble donkey.

Like the shepherds, Jesus was a nomad. He said of himself, "Foxes have dens and birds have nests, but the Son of Man has no place to lay his head" (Matthew 8:20).

Of course, the greatest symbolism is the sacred love between shepherd and those they tended, the giving of common comforts to protect something that couldn't defend itself. Shepherds possessed a willingness to risk everything for something incredibly undeserving.

If I'm honest, I recognize that this gift—this Good Shepherd coming to lay his life down for me—can't fully penetrate my understanding, probably because I'm too close to see it for what it really is. Once I step back, the image becomes much clearer. If you find yourself in my shoes, let me share a story that gave me a better understanding of my Good Shepherd.

Years ago, I helped facilitate mission trips in Juarez, Mexico. We didn't have cell phones back then, so our staff relied on walkie-talkies. We were taught to guard them with our lives, especially since things in that part of the country were known to grow legs and disappear.

One day, while our group hiked and I sat with a few of the participants who were too winded to finish the climb, a man robbed me at gunpoint. He grabbed for my walkie-talkie, but I kept fighting to hold onto it until a thought occurred to me: he had a gun and I didn't. I let go. Fear and panic swept over me, only to be overcome by the mantra my boss drilled into me: guard the walkie-talkie at all costs. So, being the obedient employee I was, I set off running after the man.

Yes, yes, I know what you're thinking: what in the world could I possibly do empty-handed against someone wielding a gun? It took me a minute to come to that same conclusion. I turned around and gave up. But the giving up part isn't the point. It's the chasing after a stupid walkie-talkie at the risk of my life. It goes without saying it wasn't worth it. It just plain didn't make sense.

Just like it doesn't make sense that a shepherd—a human!—would put their life in danger to protect a little bleating animal. Just like it makes even less sense that Jesus would give up the sweet fellowship of His Father in heaven to walk our streets in a lowly fashion and offer His life as a means of reconciling us.

So when you look at a nativity scene this year with the shepherds pushed to the back and nearly out of view, give those humble people who offered their lives a second thought and let them remind you of the One who offered His life for you.

"I am the good shepherd. The good shepherd lays down his life for the sheep."
John 10:11

# Stop and Savor

1) Imagine being one of the shepherds on the outskirts of the city as the angels sang, "Glory to God in the highest heaven, and on earth peace to those on whom his favor rests" (Luke 2:14). How would you have responded? What did the shepherds do? Read Luke 2 for the answer.

2) What are you doing this month that will foreshadow the coming year? Are you overspending on presents and will be stressed out the next few months as you try paying them off? Will excessive cookie-eating prompt a resolution to lose weight? Are you loving others lavishly, or is a bitter attitude going to start the new year with strained relationships?

3) Do you feel like a shepherd, lowly in stature (and I'm not talking about your height)? Are you scared to tell others about this magnificent gift of Messiah? Will you let the shepherd's reaction foreshadow yours?

"So they hurried off and found Mary and Joseph, and the baby, who was lying in the manger. When they had seen him, **they spread the word concerning what had been told them about this child**, and all who heard it were amazed at what the shepherds said to them."

Luke 2:16-18, emphasis mine

# December 14th

## Daring to Ask

"Mom, could you get me a plastic bin to separate my beads for Christmas?" my daughter asked.

"Mama, will you please get me a green scooter?" my six-year-old Bubba inquired.

I smiled at both appeals, trying to answer in a way that made them know I heard their requests without giving away the fact that I already planned on getting them those things.

Gabe has wanted a two-wheeled scooter for quite some time; you know, the big-boy variety rather than the three-wheeled Spiderman version he got back when he was "little." He's growing, as are his tastes. Spidey has been sitting unused for quite some time now, that extra wheel seemingly proclaiming to all that Gabe is a baby.

Micayla loves making various crafts, yet she struggles with organization almost as much as I do. There have been too many battles of bead vs. vacuum (and let's just say that the day the beads win and my newest vacuum dies will be a sad day for both of us). I want her to be creative and artistic, but

I also want to be able to walk into her room without yelping in pain after stepping on another pesky bead.

Bottom line: both of my kids' requests made perfect sense. They were asking for things well within my budget and for things I knew would benefit them. So I tried hiding my grin so they wouldn't know those items had been on my list for several months.

I had to chuckle at my own similarity. This morning before getting out of bed, part of my prayer included asking God if He would provide me with a little bit of encouragement. *I haven't gotten any e-mails from publishers saying they want to print my work lately. I know you don't have to, but if you could just send something my way that reminds me why I do this, a little push to keep going.*

In a career filled with countless rejections, sometimes my insecurities take over as I crave some extra Godly reassurance.

Thirty minutes later, I realized God probably was chuckling at me. I checked my e-mail and found a message from someone in Saudi Arabia. A man had read a story of mine in a book that had just come out, and he found me online to tell me how much it inspired him. As his words settled in, I knew it surpassed the stroke of encouragement I prayed for, especially as I thought about the fact that he contacted me through my web site (meaning he had the opportunity to read my blog and devotionals although the story that caused him to find me appeared in a secular book). Amazement coursed through my veins at the thought that a little ditty about getting a fire extinguisher for Christmas one year (sound familiar?) might have prompted this person in the Middle East to receive the word of God.

I tend to present my requests to God in the most sheepish of manners, asking for much less than what I really want, all the while hoping He won't smote me midsentence. Yet when it comes to listening to my kids' requests, especially those that will bring them more fulfillment or allow them to serve others better, I can't help but jump in and do whatever I can to make that a reality.

It seems childish to climb onto a stranger's lap dressed in a suit and fake beard to ask for something audacious. But to choose to not climb into the arms of love and ask for something that will bring God glory? That is even more childish and irrational. Let's dare to ask!

# Stop and Savor

1)  Are you asking for anything this Christmas? If so, what? (I can inquire since it's on paper. I don't dare say it in person anymore because once I asked that very question during a Christmas talk and someone replied, "a toilet seat." Trust me, it was downhill from there!).

2)  "Dream bigger, child. Dream bigger," echoes through my soul lately. Perhaps in this case we could change it to "Ask bigger. No, bigger yet." You got the safe requests out above, toilet seats and all. Now let's hear the big dreams, the bold requests.

    This isn't a name-it-and-claim-it deal. Dream big and ask big to bring glory to an even bigger God. Here's what his son said:

    "You did not choose me, but I chose you and appointed you so that you might go and bear fruit—fruit that will last—and so that whatever you ask in my name the Father will give you."

~ John 15:16

# December 15th

## Disappointed

"Christmas is going to be awful this year. I'm not getting anything good," Micayla, my ten-year-old, said.

She is grossly mistaken and yet dead-on. The first error is thinking the ultimate measurement of Christmas depends upon what she wakes up to that morning. The second is that by saying she's not getting anything good, she presumes she knows what she's getting, which she doesn't. I've found some amazing deals on things she's going to just go crazy over.

And yet.

She'll open her presents, and if I know my girl, she'll be excited. At first. But then she'll start thinking about what her friends will be getting. The game of comparisons won't take long to determine a loser and the disappointment will settle in.

Even though I'll disagree with her attitude, it will actually embody the meaning of Christmas. Yes, there was disappointment surrounding the birth of Christ. We think of shepherds being stunned and maybe even cows drawing closer to see the Messiah, but the reality is very few were impressed. In fact, most were disappointed.

The Jews faced extreme persecution. I won't detail the extremes taken against them, saving those of you who might have just eaten. Grotesque doesn't even begin to describe it.

I'd imagine that as the persecution increased, so did their hopes. Clinging to the promises penned in what we now call the Old Testament, they believed the Messiah would be a mighty king.

> "The days are coming,' declares the Lord, 'when I will raise up for David a righteous Branch, a King who will reign wisely and do what is just and right in the land.' "
> Jeremiah 23:5

They expected a king who would sit on the throne and free them from the terror they faced. Perhaps even inflict it on those who had persecuted them.

They did receive a king. A Prince of Peace. Yet he came in the form of a baby. Born to an unknown woman in a dirty stable.

Some grasped the grandeur and understood. They were among the few. The rest, well, they stood in line after the holiday, hoping to return the gift they'd long awaited for, yet found no use for.

It was a gift that couldn't be returned, a present that still doesn't make sense to our world, yet still has the power to change it–and us!

---

## Disappointment embodies the meaning of Christmas.

---

So when my daughter tells me of her disappointment, I won't chastise her. Instead, I'll just grin and say, "Let me tell you about some other people who were disappointed . . ."

# Stop and Savor

1) What would you expect if you heard a king was coming? What are some of the words that might describe him?

2) Read Jeremiah 23:5. How is Jesus, the prophesied king, depicted?

3) Based on your answers above, do you think Jesus met most people's expectations? If not, what emotions might people have felt, not just on Christmas Day, but for years, or perhaps centuries?

4) Even if you think Jeremiah 23:5 led to people hoping for something other than what they received, do you think it's an accurate representation of Jesus? Do you think He reigns wisely—even in the leading and directing of your life?

# December 16th

## Bursting and Spilling

"Mom, can't I just give you a hint of what I got you for Christmas?" Micayla asked in bubbling excitement. She loves gifts so much—both giving and receiving them—that it takes every effort for her not to tell me what I'll find under the tree. I've learned that even her hints are too revealing with the hopes that I'll guess what she got me.

I grow impatient trying to teach my kids the virtue of patience. They rarely ask, "Are we there yet?" or "How much longer?" knowing my answer will have more to do with waiting than telling them an actual time or day. It's an entirely different story, however, when it comes to Micayla's enthusiasm about gift-giving. I revel in her joy, grateful that she doesn't view the holiday as merely a day to receive.

Perhaps what I most love about watching her is the way it demonstrates the true meaning of Christmas. No, I'm not referring about the cliché of giving versus receiving. I'm talking about the fanfare, the anticipation in the giver as they think about how much you will adore the thing they purposefully selected for you, a gift so phenomenal it just might change your life.

If Micayla gets this excited over something she picked up for me at a dollar store, imagine how God felt from the beginning of time, knowing exactly what He would give the world. Is it any wonder He allowed so many prophecies to be spoken about the Messiah's birth, the gift that was long-awaited by both the receivers *and* the giver?

# Stop and Savor

1) What is the best present you gave someone? Were you anxious to give it to them? Did you drop hints about it?

2) What are some of the things that God was "bursting and spilling" about centuries before Christ's birth? The following verses give a sampling of these prophecies:
   - Isaiah 7:14
   - Micah 5:2; Matthew 2:6
   - Hosea 11:1; Matthew 2:15

3) Ephesians 1:5 says, "God decided in advance to adopt us into his own family by bringing us to himself through Jesus Christ. This is what he wanted to do, and it gave him **great pleasure**" (NLT, emphasis mine). Have you ever thought about God taking great pleasure in something?

What do you think about the fact that "God decided in advance to adopt us into his own family" by sending Jesus Christ to earth?

4) How do you feel knowing that giving you the gift of Jesus gave God great pleasure?

# December 17th

## Love in a Package

"Mom, who are all of the presents for?" my daughter asked as I carried a load of groceries in from the car.

"What are you talking about?"

"You know, the presents that are all over the kitchen counters and under the tree."

"Huh?" I muttered as I went to investigate these alleged gifts. I walked into the main area of our living space and gasped. Presents of various sizes and colors littered our place. Gift bags with tissue paper were nestled under our tiny tree. A few small gifts hung from the branches. More packages lined the counters. Everywhere I looked, presents abounded.

"Mom, where did these come from?" Micayla repeated.

"I'm not sure, sweet girl," I replied as we looked at the gifts.

I heard a rumor that some friends were going to do the 12 days of Christmas for me, but I forgot about it until I saw those bags lining my kitchen counters and perched under my tree. I shooed the kids upstairs and dropped to my knees in tears. I didn't know who was part of "elfing" me, but I knew there were quite a few involved, especially in figuring out how to get them *inside* my house while I was gone.

Although I didn't know who they were from, I knew exactly what was inside those beautiful packages. Some had been filled with chocolate, my all-time favorite food, or at least they had been before my black lab found them (which was why they were on the counters rather than under the tree). But chocolate or not, I knew what was inside *all* of the packages. I didn't have to open them to know what it was, for it was obvious.

They were filled with love.

I collapsed to the floor, grateful for such incredible friends, yet also amazed to see something I'd completely overlooked.

Love.

I knew Christmas wasn't about the gifts. Instead, I thought it was about: a baby, a beautiful giving of life to prevent our death, the miraculous, and about prophecies fulfilled. But those were by-products. The real gift was love.

Maybe you've always seen it, the love in the gift. Or perhaps you've been more like me, savoring the gift without truly relishing the motive behind it. No matter which category you're in, you are loved. Deeply so. Cherish that truth. Relish it like a steaming cup of coffee on a cold morning, warming first your face and then your insides. It bears repeating. You are loved. I am loved. More vastly than we could even begin to fathom.

---

## The real gift of Christmas is love.

No matter how many or few presents are under your tree, there is one that can change your entire life: love in a package.

# Stop and Savor

1) What do you think Joseph was most in need of after learning that Mary was pregnant? What emotions do you think he felt? What were some of the first words the angel said to him in Matthew 1:20? How could those words be a demonstration of God's love and concern for Joseph?

2) There is a tradition saying that priests tied a rope to their ankle before entering the Holy of Holies in case God struck them dead. Imagine Zechariah's shock as he stood in the temple of the Lord and was greeted by Gabriel. What gifts of love did Gabriel give him in Luke 1:11-17?

3) What are you going to do with this gift of love that is given to you? Are you going to embrace it? Will you share it with others, either by telling

your friends about the incredible gift of Jesus, or by loving them in a deeper, more authentic way?

# December 18<sup>th</sup>

## The Wisdom of the Wise

They were the sages of the day. I envision them like professors nearing retirement, men whose vast knowledge was only rivaled by their deep-seated wisdom. The original color of their hair had long since been replaced with tufts of grey in the places where hair remained.

Yes, the wise men were proclaimed to be just that, wise, yet the limited knowledge we have about them defies all stereotypes I hold of scholars. For years they traveled with nothing more than a star directing them. Yes, years. Two, in fact.

Imagine the conversation as they'd stop at night (or would it be during the day so they could see the bright guiding light in the dark?) and ask for a place to sleep.

"Sure, you can stay at my inn. Where are you headed, anyways?"

"Well, we don't know for sure. We're just following that star."

"A star, huh? How long have you been doing this?"

"This is day 432."

Can't you see the inn-keeper trying to suppress a smile as he thinks the hot weather was wreaking havoc on the so-called wise men?

Fast-forward a bit. "They went on their way, and the star they had seen when it rose went ahead of them until it stopped over the place where the child was. When they saw the star, they were overjoyed" (Matthew 2:9-10). The English Standard Version translates it this way: "When they saw the star, they rejoiced exceedingly with great joy."

Can you picture it, these wise folks rejoicing over a *star*! It wasn't a "hey, look, we finally made it" celebration, either. This was an all-out "exceedingly joyful" event. It doesn't fit what I'd expect magi to do.

I went to a Christmas concert a few years ago. After singing a heartfelt song penned in reverence to the newborn Messiah, the artist then asked the audience to join him in singing Jingle Bells. There were a few kids scattered throughout the crowd, all of whom jumped at the chance to be part of a sing along. The rest of the group just sat there awkwardly, looking from one person to the next with an expression that asked one and all: does he really expect us to be enthusiastic about a children's song? Throughout the next few minutes, the magic of Christmas gave way to nervous glances. *Surely grown adults aren't going to act so foolish*, we secretly thought.

The wise men weren't above traveling for years to find a baby, and they weren't too cool to rejoice abundantly when they found that small child. They broke the stereotypical norms, and as a result, they found Jesus.

We'd be wise to follow their example.

# Stop and Savor

1) When, if ever, did you rejoice at the deepest level over Christ's birth?

2) Is there anything you've ever wanted to do to celebrate Christmas, but never did because you thought others might look at you funny or it just felt too out of character? Perhaps you've wanted to fall to your knees in worship during a Christmas Eve service, or cry tears of "great joy," yet never did.

3) What might happen if you followed the wisemen's lead and did something out of character, something that might require a good deal of time or resources, or something that might look as goofy as an overly excited professor in order to celebrate the King?

# December 19th

## X Marks the Spot

Some have devoted their entire beings to the letter "X", spending all of their time and energy in an attempt to find it. Others have literally given their lives for it, their endeavors ending in death. Movies highlight the heroism of many who have struggled to find this letter. Indiana Jones searched for it in caves and temples. Captain Jack Sparrow sought it out at the *Isla de Muerta* (the island of death).

---

Rather than being offended at the abbreviation X, we can use it as a reminder to pursue Christ.

---

Armed with a treasure map, pirates and archaeologists risk everything to find the coveted spot designated with an "X." We marvel at their courage, yet sometimes get upset when others talk about "X" by writing Merry Xmas.

The Greek word for Christ is *Χριστός*. Its abbreviated form is "X." During the 16<sup>th</sup> century, people began substituting this abbreviated Greek word into the name of the winter holiday. Merry Xmas had nothing to do with removing Christ from Christmas. Rather than being offended at the abbreviation, we can use it as a reminder to pursue X—Christ—as relentlessly as Indiana Jones sought the Holy Grail.

# Stop and Savor

1) What is something you pursued valiantly? Did you find it? If so, how did you feel once you did? If you didn't find it, what made you stop your quest?

2) Do you realize it is only through Christ that you can unearth the greatest treasure of all time?

3) Will you search for Christ as if your very life depends upon it? What steps can you take to seek out Christ more?

# December 20<sup>th</sup>

## The Forgotten Ornament

Two friends and I decided to meet for breakfast a few weeks before Christmas.

"Let's bring ornaments for each other," one friend (let's call her Beth) suggested.

"Sounds great," we all agreed.

We showed up at the restaurant Monday morning. Jody and I put on our gift bags on the table and began chatting until Beth arrived.

"Oh, no!" Beth screamed when she got to our table. "I totally forgot the ornaments!" Her face turned several shades of red after realizing she forgot to buy the very thing she suggested we all exchange.

So what did we do?

Did I give Jody an extra ornament instead of letting Beth have it? Did Jody and I send Beth home and refuse to let her eat with us or demand that she pick up ornaments later in the day and drop them off to us? Or did we just laugh about it, telling her countless times to not worry about it as she brought it up yet again?

## Savoring Christmas

It was easy to laugh it off, in large part because Beth is a fun-loving lady, but also because I've been there before more times than I can remember. The guilt settles deep whenever I receive a gift from someone I never thought of buying something for. But this experience allowed me to clearly see it from the other person's point of view.

Beth is one of my all-time favorite people. I'm honored to walk this journey of life with her, and was ecstatic when I found an ornament that reflected a huge accomplishment she attained the prior year. I had been waiting for weeks to see her open it and hadn't thought for even a second about what type of ornament she might get me. Why? Because it didn't matter!

That morning prepared me for the phone call I received two days later. Emma, a dear, sweet grandma that I get to see much too infrequently called saying she had a little something for the kids and me and wanted to know if we could get together that afternoon. Time with Emma is a treat, so I hopped in the shower since I had just gone on a long run, picked the kids up from school and trekked to Starbucks.

We embraced in a group hug when we walked in the door, my head furrowed against her beautiful grey hair while the kids gripped her knees. Time slowed as we chatted and laughed. It was a tremendous gift, one I was very lucky to receive.

We later said our good-byes and headed to the parking lot, where Emma pulled out a large black trash bag. "Don't wait until Christmas to open this. You can open it tonight or tomorrow," she said with a smile. "Some of it is for you, and some is for the the rest of your family. You'll figure it out."

I pulled the contents out that evening. Inside the bag were tears: mine, that is. I cried those sweet drops of liquid that can only come from the astonishment of knowing that someone cared *that much*.

There was a warm, fuzzy blanket for each of us, something I had wished for just the week before as the kids and I tried sharing a blanket while watching a movie. It was supposed to a fun family evening, yet the tugs on the lone piece of fabric began stretching our compassion for each other. *How could she possibly have known that I wanted another blanket?*

There was a book on hearing God even in trying times, a read that provided many of the answers I most desperately needed during that particular season of life. An envelope lingered at the bottom, lined with one piece of currency I had never touched prior to that day, let alone received. Awe coursed through my veins in utter disbelief.

There was no way I could repay such kindness. In fact, I knew any attempts of doing so would diminish the purpose and heart behind

Emma's gifts. When I called her the next day, she simply said, "I know you've been going through a tough time and I just wanted to do a little something."

As I type these words, I sit wrapped in my blanket of compassion and love. I can't repay this. Nor will I try. I don't deserve it in the least, but I will accept it with gratitude, joy, and of course, more tears.

We will soon be celebrating a day that is all about a gift given in love, sacrifice, and generosity. None of us will ever work hard enough to earn it, nor will we ever be good enough to deserve it. We can reject the gift because we don't deserve it. Or we can embrace our unworthiness and let it make us savor the gift that much more. Which will you choose?

# Stop and Savor

1) Have you ever forgotten to get someone a gift, but they gave you one? If so, how did that make you feel?

2) Have you ever received something you didn't think you were worthy of? Did you use the present, or did you put it aside simply because it was too lavish?

3) Do something today that causes you to thank God more frequently. For example, you could use Christmas ornaments to be a reminder to stop and say thanks, or offer up a short prayer of thanksgiving every time you hear a Christmas carol today.

# December 21st

## I Am Gabriel

The "problem" with naming your son Gabriel is that he might think he's an angel. My Gabriel is awfully sweet and adorable, but I assure you he's no angel!

Every year as he sets up the nativity, he saves the angel for last. "There I am," he beams as he places it on top. His "that's me" perspective has caused some interesting conversations: "So, tell us what it was like on the night Jesus was born."

He has the most fantastic, vivid imagination, yet I'm not about to share his responses. Instead, I'll let it intrigue you like it did me with the hopes that you will create your own image of what Gabriel might have witnessed.

I imagine Gabriel looking at Mary after telling her his incredible news, her eyes wide with shock and disbelief. I visualize grandeur mixed with a serene acceptance and awe. I see Joseph trying to help deliver the One who would deliver him. I picture him feeling out of place, uncertain how to deliver a baby and best help his young wife. I see him with that awkward first-time dad, shoulders hunched stature, petrified of breaking God's Redeemer.

My mind can conjure many things, many of which I'm sure are completely inaccurate, but there's one thing I can't begin to picture:

"I am Gabriel. **I stand in the presence of God**, and I have been sent to speak to you and to tell you this good news." Luke 1:19, emphasis mine

Pretend to be my Bubba, err, I mean, Gabriel. What might you see if you stood in the presence of God? While the questions above are nothing more than speculative, there will be a day when we can fully know what it's like to stand in God's presence! Isn't that a most baffling, wondrous thought?

Before you start mentally listing off reasons that disqualify you from heaven, let me assure you of the only thing needed to join Gabriel in the heavenly throne room:

"If you confess with your mouth the Lord Jesus and believe in your heart that God has raised Him from the dead, you will be saved." Romans 10:9, NKJV

# Stop and Savor

1) What do you think Gabriel saw as he talked to Mary?

2) What sort of facial expressions do you think Mary exhibited:

- At the sight of an angel?
- At the news of hearing she was pregnant?
- After hearing she was going to give birth to the Messiah?

3) What do you think Gabriel saw as the Christ child entered our world?

# December 22nd

## Lavish

I never baked cookies last Christmas. Cards never crossed my mind. I couldn't even give my friends small gifts due to a shrinking budget.

Despite my lack of giving, I received more than ever before. It started when I returned home from a friend's house, only to find my kitchen counters lined with presents (the counters because apparently my dog had already helped herself to some of the edible presents, causing the unknown delivery person to move them higher). Each item had a number on it, along with a set of simple instructions: start with day one and open one thing every day.

I say one thing, but really it was more like one gift bag or one box, filled with gift cards to grocery stores, Starbucks, and even a few cards to restaurants for the nights I didn't want to cook. Someone gave my son an educational but fun game, a thoughtful gift for my Bubba who struggles in school. Another "elf" gave my daughter red velvet hot chocolate (a variation of her favorite type of cake) and an i-tunes gift card since she loves music. I received various types of dark chocolate, which in my book is really the only kind that matters.

We didn't get scraps. Every day for twelve days, we received things that we truly needed, as well as luxuries that were hand-picked for us. Many adjectives ran through my head throughout those twelve days, words such as amazing, generous, and thoughtful, but it was on day thirteen that I thought back over all the gifts we had received and I could sum them up in one profound word: lavish.

My friends knew I was going through a rough period and they wanted to do a little something to help out. What they couldn't have known is they surpassed their goal: they didn't do anything little, and they didn't just give me a few things.

They lavished us with community. Encouragement. Love. Prayer. Support. Even faith.

Whether or not people "elf" you or you find a single present under the tree with your name on it, you, too, have been showered with love, for that is what Christmas is about. It is an over-the-top, incomprehensible love extended to you and to me.

And the best part is, it lasts much longer than twelve days!

# Stop and Savor

1) Have you ever felt like someone lavished you with something? It could be a Christmas present, something you received unexpectedly during the year, or a million different things. If so, how did it make you feel?

2) Have you ever received something that you hadn't asked for, but it was exactly what you wanted?

3) Reread the previous questions. Could Jesus' love be the answer to both of those questions?

"See what great love the Father has lavished on us, that we should be called children of God! And that is what we are! The reason the world does not know us is that it did not know him" (1 John 3:1).

# December 23rd

## Toy Store Tantrums

"Christmas is soooooooooo far away," my five-year old wailed as I peeled him off the floor in the toy department. The days of waiting were just too much for him. He grew tired of knowing that many of the things on the shelves he longed for might be under the tree for him. He wanted them that instant.

Prophets told of Christ's birth. Hopes were raised. Anticipation grew. And grew. And then perhaps, it nearly died. 400 long years of silence can have that effect. Nearly 150,000 days. 3.5 million hours.

I remember when my Girlie was little and I knew my parents were coming to visit. I couldn't tell her when they left their house, for she could easily ask if they were at my place yet over 1,000 times in the 20 minutes it took them to make the drive. Instead, I had to wait until just a few minutes before I expected them, and even then we had to dash down our apartment stairs and start walking through the parking lot to the front entrance so we wouldn't have to wait the few extra seconds for them to drive to our building.

I couldn't blame her for being so excited to see them: the moments of expectation and longing were just too much for her to handle.

The moments.

Not the hours, months, or decades the Israelites experienced. 400 long years filled with expectation and then extreme hardship and persecution. 3.5 million *hours!*

That's fertile ground for a phrase to be birthed long before the advent of road-trips: *How much longer?*

As my Bubba started flailing on the ground, a grin erupted over my face as I realized that out-of-control body encompassed an aspect of the meaning of Christmas.

Who knows? One day I just might get down on the toy store floor with him and say, "Let me tell you about other people that had to wait for Christmas . . ."

## Stop and Savor

1) Think about a time you had to wait for something much longer than you expected. How did you handle it? Did you grow more excited, become frustrated, or give up hope altogether?

2) What things are you still waiting on? Maybe it's for God to provide you with a spouse, heal you from a disease, or just for the opportunity to see Him face to face. How are you handling your wait?

3) Does your strength disappear after waiting a while? If so, read Isaiah 40:31. What connection do you notice between hope and strength?

# December 24ᵗʰ

## Ceasing to Expect

I could say I don't expect anything for Christmas, but that isn't fully true. I've come to expect my mom to call me a few weeks before Christmas to plan a little shopping trip. We normally head to a clothing store and I pick out a sweater or two. Then she takes the items home, wraps them, and gives them to me Christmas day. I would still love my parents just as much if they didn't get me anything, but it has become such a pattern that a lack of gifts would make me wonder if I did something to upset them.

I've also come to expect the tin of cookies that my aunt stuffs with her delicious baked goods every year. It is obviously a labor of love as the container is filled to the hilt with every kind of sweet you can imagine. There are sugar cookies, hand-made candy, chocolate chip cookies, and at least twenty other types of yumminess. She even includes a jar or two of her homemade hot pepper jelly, made with peppers she grows earlier in the year. My kids have come to expect that if they ask if a certain kind of cookie is good, I'll more adamantly declare it's awful if it's one of my favorites (yes, I'm still disappointed that they figured out my little trick. No more of my aunt's incredible baklava for me!).

Last year, the expectation ended, or more aptly, I received things I never could have expected. Those little elves who snuck into my house helped me realize that I had come to expect certain things. As a result, I didn't value them as much as if I didn't know they were coming.

But to walk into my house and see the counters lined with presents? How could anyone ever expect that?

In fact, I had to send my kids to a friend's house for a bit while I stared at the many gifts and cried. I didn't even know what was inside those gift bags and boxes, yet I fully understood that it was something I didn't deserve. Something I hadn't done anything to merit.

I pinched myself repeatedly during those twelve days, shaking my head in disbelief that others cared so much about my family and me that they would go to great lengths for us.

The presents lasted twelve days, but the deep-seated feeling of receiving extravagant gifts of love lasted longer.

But not much.

I write this seven months later, those gift cards a distant memory. I'm still touched, yet the sense of awe and appreciation has faded.

Perhaps that, too, is Christmas. We know December 25$^{th}$ will come as surely as my beautiful Rocky Mountains will continue to be majestic. We can guarantee that children will race down the stairs, and many adults will stop for a moment to ponder and appreciate the birth of the Christ-child who came for our sins. Maybe the appreciation will sink deep; will mesmerize us, revolutionize us. Transform us.

At least for twelve or so days.

But what if we removed the expectation for just a bit? What if we no longer approached Christmas with the same assurance that I had knowing a purple sweater—the very one I picked out with my mom—would be under the tree? What if we stopped viewing the season as something we know without a doubt will come, and instead stop and remember that none of it was merited?

What if we viewed it like I did those counters overflowing with gifts, as we drop to our knees, flood our eyes with tears, and reflect upon how fortunate we are? What if we could cease to expect, and in the process come to appreciate and revel in the gift more than ever before?

# Stop and Savor

1) Do you have any expectations of Christmas? If so, what are they? It could be that you anticipate receiving a certain number of presents, or envision having the same meal you have every Christmas.

2) What can you do for someone else today that is totally unexpected? Could you shovel a neighbor's drive or phone a friend who needs a listening ear?

3) It's impossible to remove the expectation for something we know is coming. However, we can ask God to instill in us a desire to appreciate the deepest meaning of Christmas without all of the fluff or stress of the season. Spend some time in prayer thanking God for His gift, as well as

asking Him to help you revel in the most selfless gift ever given: Jesus Christ.

# December 25th

## No Forwarding Address

My husband, a mailman, goes missing every December. Cold, wintry conditions and increased volume make for long days. The number of packages needing to be delivered rises, as does the volume of cards. Red and green envelopes fill his satchel, many of which are addressed to people he knows haven't lived at that location for months or even years. Most are forwarded, but many of these annual "catch-up" letters are returned to the sender with the intended recipients never receiving them.

Some of us live in a way that mimics those cards. We might not have a close relationship with God. Perhaps guilt drives us to church on Christmas and Easter, a sort of "Here I am, God" letter being sent to the heavenlies. Others of us might drift away, unwittingly turning from God's will to ours. We might stop sending "letters," those prayers of adoration or petitions for help.

Yet no matter what we have or haven't done, one fact remains: God doesn't need a forwarding address. Jesus himself said, "For the Son of Man came to seek and to save the lost" (Luke 19:10). Did you catch that? To *seek*, like a letter sent with specific instructions to find the addressee at all costs rather than returning it to the sender.

There have been many instances when I receive a Christmas card from someone I didn't send one to. I usually feel embarrassed and regretful. I wonder if I've hit the magic limit as to when it's too late to send a card (or too obvious that I'm sending one in response to receiving something from that person). But no matter what, I always, *always* open their card.

I hope you do too, for if you haven't read it recently, there is a letter with your name on it.

---

"For the Son of Man came to seek and to save the lost."
Luke 19:10

---

# Stop and Savor

1) If you sent out cards this year or last, how many of them came back to you? If some came back, how did it make you feel?

2) How do you feel when you receive a Christmas card from a friend you haven't heard from in a while?

3) Where are you at with your "Christmas cards" between you and God? If you haven't "sent" him one in a while, it isn't too late. Now might be a good time to stop and say a short prayer to Him.

# December 26th

## Post-Christmas Thoughts

## The Urgent Non-Verbal Cue

My guess is you've seen it before. Maybe you've even given it yourself. Perhaps you created a signal or learned a bit of sign language to convey a vital action to someone. This urgent non-verbal cue is recognizable from afar, that sharp eye from mother to child, that desperate pleading look saying, "Please say thank you," without wanting to voice the words in front of the person who is supposed to receive the verbal acknowledgement.

This cue is urgent. Parents long for their children to be appreciative and grateful, yet this prompt typically remains non-verbal because who wants to spend their money on somebody, only to have them be reminded to stop long enough to mutter a thank you?

By now, the presents are probably opened. You might be sighing a breath of relief that you've made it through the rush, or perhaps you're grateful that the in-laws are headed back home (and out of yours!). But whatever the case, don't be like a five-year-old so desperate to play with his new Legos that he forgets to thank the person who gave them.

You might not receive any non-verbal cues, but don't let that stop you from seeing the importance in thanking God for the best Christmas present ever: His son.

What we've received is much better than a Barbie or GI Joe. Make sure to stop and say thanks.

# Stop and Savor

1) What is one of the best presents you gave someone this year? What made it special?

2) How did they receive it? Did their reaction line up with what you expected, and how did that make you feel?

3) 2 Corinthians 9:15 says, "Thanks be to God for his indescribable gift!" The psalmist wrote, "Praise the Lord. **Give thanks to the Lord**, for he is good; his love endures forever" (Psalm 106:1, emphasis mine). Stop right now. Put everything else on hold, even if only for a few seconds. Let your anthem of thanksgiving ring out for an indescribable gift.

# December 27th

## Understanding the Gift

Every once in a while I'll receive a remarkable gift, but when I first open it, I have no idea what it is or how to use it. One example occurred a few years after receiving the fire extinguisher. My parents once again beamed as I went to open a certain present. I, of course, had learned my lesson and was more cautious and reserved.

I gingerly peeled off the red and green paper to find a wooden shelf with a hole in it. I flipped it every possible angle trying to determine what it was, my best guess being it was meant to hold a baseball and a bat. That perplexed me since I was a soccer girl. My parents' grins shone bright, driving the fear in deeper.

"Can't you see? It's for your hair dryer and curling iron," they chimed in.

I am fully a child of the 80's, meaning that both of those bathroom appliances were daily essentials, along with a full bottle of Aqua Net. I used that wooden shelf every day for years, giving me a safe place to hang my curling iron after I had used it (after all, my parents didn't want to put me at risk of using that fire extinguisher!).

Once I understood the purpose of the gift, it provided tremendous value.

I write these words in the event that some of you have been reading these stories every day, laughing with me about the silly things my children do, or my odd way of looking at things, yet you still find yourself turning the gift over and over, trying to make sense of what exactly it is and how it fits your life.

My words are going to fall short here. You will still turn the present over and over and have questions. That is inevitable, in part because that is actually a portion of the gift. God gives us the ability to think critically and ask countless questions without Him getting upset or agitated.

So while I can't fully explain this present, I will offer you this: it is the gift of love given for you. Jesus gave up the grandeur and beauty of heaven to come live on earth for you and for me.

The first part of Romans 6:23 shows us the consequences of sin. It says, "The wages of sin is death." Note that *sin* is singular. Just one sin and we're doomed.

We would miss so much if we only looked at the first part of the verse, for the second half gives us a rich promise. The entire verse reads "The wages of sin is death, but the gift of God is eternal life in Christ Jesus our Lord."

Did you catch that? You have been offered a gift—the treasure of eternal life. If you begin this faith-walk, you will no longer have to wonder what will happen to you once your earthly body dies. Instead, you can have full assurance of spending eternity in heaven!

So how does one go about receiving this gift? It is easier than you might think. Romans 9:9 says, "If you declare with your mouth, 'Jesus is Lord,' and believe in your heart that God raised him from the dead, you will be saved."

I knew someone who received a Christmas card from his parents when he was in high school. He opened it in haste, threw it in the fireplace, and grabbed the next item. The problem was, he did all of it in such a hurry that he didn't realize there was a hundred dollar bill in that card.

What he didn't know cost him. The same is true of what he didn't appreciate or take the time to embrace.

I hope the same won't be true of you.

# Stop and Savor

1) How well do you feel like you understand the gift of the Messiah coming to earth for us?

2) Romans 9:9 says, "If you declare with your mouth, 'Jesus is Lord,' and believe in your heart that God raised him from the dead, you will be saved." If you haven't made that declaration before, now might be a good time! Here's a prayer you could pray:

> *Jesus, I know I'm a sinner—that I goof up and do things wrong. Please forgive me. I also know that you came to save me. Even though I'll never fully understand how or why you did that, thank you. I believe you died to take away my sins. I also believe you rose again. I invite you into my heart. Please teach me your ways. Amen.*

If you previously made this declaration, stop once again to thank Christ for the remarkable gift and sacrifice He paid on your behalf.

3) What steps can you take in the coming year to deepen your understanding of this gift? If you're looking for a way to study the Bible, feel free to check out the Studying the Bible pdf on the free resources tab of my website (www.stacyvoss.com).

# December 28th

## White Christmas

We dream of it and Bing Crosby sang of it. Some of us hoped for it this year, and others of us knew that little white flakes would never frequent our part of the country.

Why all the fanfare for a White Christmas?

Perhaps it is because the gift given on that first Christmas is the only thing that can turn our crimson sins whiter than snow.

---

The gift given on that first Christmas is the only thing that can turn our crimson sins whiter than snow.

---

# Stop and Savor

1) Did you hope for a white Christmas this year? Did you get one?

2) Write out Psalm 51:7 below or on a note card.

3) How does that verse impact you?

4) Every time you see snow, let it be a reminder of the price Jesus paid for you to be whiter than snow.

# December 29th

## One Size Doesn't Fit All

OSFA. That's what the tag in my robe said. One Size Fits All. A universal measuring rod designed to fit every size and shape. All except me, that is. The robe apparently was designed to be short. Pair that with my long legs and you can (literally) see the problem!

If we glance too quickly at the manger, we might think it has OSFA written all over it. After all, there was one tiny baby that came to earth to save all. Although all can be saved through the gift that arrived that first Christmas, it isn't OSFA.

Here's the truth: Jesus doesn't fit everyone. Some will love and adore him. Others will think he was a good person, but nothing more. But it goes much, much further than that. If we view the Christ-child as the robe that hopefully is big enough to cover all of mankind, we fall horribly short. It is only once we see Him as the gift sent to redeem and transform us that we can recognize how personal and undying that love truly is. And that can never be found with a One Size Fits All tag on it.

# Stop and Savor

1) Have you ever visited a friend or gone to a hotel where you felt like special attention was taken in preparing your room? What happened? Was there a mint on your pillow at night, fresh-baked cookies or a plush robe? Describe what set that experience apart from others.

2) Think about your dream place. Is it a condo, a beach house, a mountain cabin? Does anything hang from the walls? Are there any special scents or foods in it?

3) Jesus said, "My Father's house has many rooms; if that were not so, would I have told you that I am going there to prepare a place for you?" (John 14:2).

How does it make you feel knowing that heaven isn't One Size Fits All; that every room is specifically prepared for its intended recipient? How does it feel to know that Jesus is preparing your place?

4) Is there anything special you think you'll find in your room in heaven? I wouldn't be surprised if mine has a fountain of dark chocolate that never stops (or stains!), as well as a mini trampoline since I'm a bit too energetic, especially after drinking from chocolate fountains. What might be waiting in your room?

# December 30th

## Are We Lost?

"Are we lost?" my grandma asked my dad while he was driving.

"No, I know where we're going," he politely responded to his future mother-in-law.

A few minutes passed, along with multiple turns here and there.

"Now are we lost?" my grandma questioned again.

"No!" Dad responded, this time with a little more oomph. "I'll get us there."

The questioning continued, along with my dad's insistence on knowing his way.

"Rick," my mom quietly whispered. "Just admit you're lost."

"Okay," he muttered, trying to appease both his pride and future bride. "We're lost."

"Oh, goody!" my grandma cheerfully quipped. "Now we can dig into our 'we're lost' bag!" She began opening bag of chips, cookies and all sorts of "emergency" junk food.

Her reaction surprised my dad since at that time he didn't fully understand my grandma's spunky outlook. What he thought would bring ridicule was actually cause for a celebration.

I tend to live like that, too. I fear admitting my true condition—of feeling lost, turned around, or maybe even a little hopeless. I naively believe that if I do, others will judge and condemn.

Many feel lost and confused this time of year: unsure how to pay off the growing bills, hurt by what did or did not transpire on Christmas, lost in loneliness, and so much more.

We can keep these feelings to ourselves, tucked deep inside where they will fester and grow.

I wasn't being fully honest when I said I was naïve to believe some will judge and condemn me if I let them know of my hurts, fears, or uncertainties. Some will. But not God. In fact, He just might give us something beneficial in return or perhaps it will even be cause for celebration. Who knows, maybe God will break out the "someone just admitted they are lost" bag.

# Stop and Savor

1) Are you able to admit when you're lost?

2) Here's an example of Jesus giving us something opposite of what we might expect. Jesus said to not worry about tomorrow in Matthew 6:34. We might think that if we came to him exhausted or burdened, He would rebuke us for worrying, but instead He offers something else. What is it, according to Matthew 11:28? How does that make you feel?

3) Are there areas of your life or in your thinking that you've been scared to admit to God? Perhaps you feel lost in your faith or where you should go. Is it possible that God's response to

you telling Him about it might be completely different than you expect?

# December 31ˢᵗ

## May it be to Me

"Turn right in a half mile," the voice on my navigation app told me.

"But I know it's straight ahead," I said to no one in particular as I continued on my way.

Sometimes I'm convinced that the designers of GPS systems figure out ways to make people go in circles a few times. I can't remember how many times that automatic voice has instructed me to veer off the main road and take a lap through a neighborhood before telling me to get back on the same road it just led me away from.

It's caused me to lose confidence in the system. Sure, most times I rely heavily on it, yet other times I listen to the voice and laugh. "I know better," I declare as I keep the wheel set on what I believe should be my course.

Unfortunately, I have this mindset both while using my phone, as well as when I navigate this journey called life. "Turn right," I hear.

"Ha! Whatever," I respond.

"Follow me," He whispers.

"Sure, if it fits with my plans," I feel my heart respond, yet I'm too embarrassed to own my stubborn pride and truly voice it to God.

I think the first Christmas really was about GPS. We've already looked at the professors as they meandered for years to find the Christ-child. But what about Mary? Gabriel could have told her she was going to give birth to the Messiah and she easily could have say, "No way! I'm not doing *that!*"

She could have "turned off" the voice of the One leading and guiding her. "I have plans. I'm getting married soon. I have my whole life ahead of me. You've got this wrong."

But she didn't. Instead, she offered a simple plea of eloquent acceptance: "May it be to me as you have said."[3]

Our world—*and eternity!* —are different because of it.

Whether or not you received a GPS for Christmas, make sure you listen to the truest voice of navigation throughout the coming year. If it says to turn right, stop and consider before rejecting it (better yet, don't reject it at all!). Or when the gentle nudge prompts you to do something you might not otherwise, heed it.

# Stop and Savor

1) What do you do when someone (or something) gives you a direction that is opposite from what you believe to be true?

2) Have you ever had your plans interrupted, either on a short-term level or perhaps a much larger scale? If so, how did you respond?

3) Would you be willing to commit to a "may it be to me" attitude this coming year, allowing the Holy Spirit to lead and guide you? If so, write a prayer asking for God's guidance and give Him permission to interrupt your plans.

# References

## December 3<sup>rd</sup>: The Scent of Death

[1] Retrieved from http://kjanicki-sotd.blogspot.com/2010_12_01_archive.html on 1/14/14.

## December 8<sup>th</sup>: God, Sitting on a Curb

[2] Mathew 1:23

## December 31<sup>st</sup>: May it be to Me

[3] Luke 1:38.

# About the Author

Stacy Voss is a writer and speaker who encourages women on their faith walks, stimulating them to a more intimate, authentic relationship with their Creator. She is a regular contributor to Today's Christian Woman, and her work also appears in place such as *Chicken Soup for the Christmas Soul* and Dr. Gary Chapman's *Love is a Verb.*

Stacy stumbled upon a journey towards contentment several years ago, which led to her starting a gratitude revolution. She posts about gratitude at

www.facebook.com/Gratimoments.

She makes her home in Highlands Ranch, Colorado, where she spends her days keeping up with her two energetic, fun-loving kids (and her nights trying to recover!). Follow her at www.stacyvoss.com.

**ENRICHING HEARTS AND MINDS THROUGH GRATITUDE**

**Gratimoment** [grat-i- moh- m*uh* nt] noun.

1. A period of time filled with thankfulness
2. An exercise against discontentment
3. Short periods of time that can lead to a changed way of thinking and living

What exactly is a Gratimoment? It's simply a moment of gratitude, brief reprieves from the woes of the day to stop and say thanks, snapshots setting our hearts on the path to contentment.

To learn more about gratitude, discover how to cultivate and share your Gratimoments, and more, go to:

www.StacyVoss.com/Gratimoments

or

www.Gratimoment.com